Quiche Coc

Delicious Quiche Recipes that Will Create the Perfect Breakfast or Brunch Dish

BY

Stephanie Sharp

Copyright © 2019 by Stephanie Sharp

License Notes

Copyright 2019 by Stephanie Sharp All rights reserved.

No part of this Book may be transmitted or reproduced into any format for any means without the proper permission of the Author. This includes electronic or mechanical methods, photocopying or printing.

The Reader assumes all risk when following any of the guidelines or ideas written as they are purely suggestion and for informational purposes. The Author has taken every precaution to ensure accuracy of the work but bears no responsibility if damages occur due to a misinterpretation of suggestions.

My deepest thanks for buying my book! Now that you have made this investment in time and money, you are now eligible for free e-books on a weekly basis! Once you subscribe by filling in the box below with your email address, you will start to receive free and discounted book offers for unique and informative books. There is nothing more to do! A reminder email will be sent to you a few days before the promotion expires so you will never have to worry about missing out on this amazing deal. Enter your email address below to get started. Thanks again for your purchase!

Just visit the link or scan QR-code to get started!

https://stephanie-sharp.subscribemenow.com

Table of Contents

Introduction 8

    Mini-Quiche 9

    Spinach Quiche 11

    Hamburger Quiche 14

    Carrot Cashew Quiche 17

    Bean Pie 20

    Weeknight Quiche 22

    Cheddar Quiche 25

    Beef & Biscuit Pie 28

    Corn Tortilla Quiche 31

    Chiles Rellenos Pie 34

    Crab Quiche 37

    Ham & Wild Rice Quiche 40

    Mexi-Quiche 43

Morel Quiche 46

Cauliflower Cheese Pie 49

Vegetable Quiche 52

Crustless Quiche 55

BBQ Pie 58

Onion Quiche 61

Quiche Seville 63

Tomato, Kale & Leek Quiche 65

Easy Pot Pie 68

Rice Crust for Quiche 70

Salmon Quiche 72

Bacon Pie 75

Shrimp Quiche 77

Spinach Artichoke Quiche 79

Chicken Pot Pie 82

Ultimate Quiche 85

Artichoke Pie 88

Conclusion 91

About the Author 92

Author's Afterthoughts 93

Introduction

Don't you just love a good quiche? If you aren't familiar with quiches, let's pull you up to speed. A quiche is a delicious savory dish, that is made using a combination of vegetables, cheese, meats and of course eggs that create in an oven fresh custard. I can taste the deliciousness now. It originated in France and quickly traveled across the globe to be used for all occasions.

This Quiche Cookbook will be exploring 30 amazingly easy and delish Quiche recipes that you can enjoy with your whole family. So, go ahead and grab your creativity, and apron and flip the page to get started.

wwwwwwwwwwwwwwwwwwwwwwwwwwwwwwwwwwwwwwww

Mini-Quiche

Mini-Quiche recipes provide an easy and fun way to serve a delicious meal to a group of people. Take these to any party for an instant hit. You can garnish with olives!

Serving Size: 6 – 8

Total Prep Time: 30 minutes

Ingredients:

- 12 slices bread
- 1 onion, chopped
- ½ c. Swiss cheese, shredded
- 1 c. milk
- 4 eggs
- 1 tsp. dry mustard
- ¼ tsp. black pepper

Directions:

1. Preheat oven to 375 degrees. Grease 12 muffin tins

2. Cut bread into circles Place on bottoms of muffin tins. Sprinkle the onion and cheese evenly among the muffin tins.

3. Mix milk, eggs, mustard and pepper in a bowl until combined. Divide evenly amount muffin tins.

4. Bake for 20 minutes.

5. Serve and enjoy!

Spinach Quiche

This is one of the most traditional forms of quiche and is always a crowd-pleaser. It is a forgiving recipe that can be customized to your tastes and desires!

Serving Size: 6 – 8

Total Prep Time: 1 hour 18 minutes

Ingredients:

- Butter, ½ c.
- garlic, 3 tsp., minced
- onion, 1, chopped
- spinach, 1 – 10 oz. package frozen, chopped, thawed and drained
- mushroom, 1 – 4.5 oz. canned
- herb feta, 1 – 6 oz. package, crumbled
- cheddar cheese, 1 – 8 oz. package, shredded
- Salt & pepper to taste
- 9" pie crust, 1, unbaked
- eggs, 4, beaten
- milk, 1 c.

Directions:

1. Heat oven to 375 degrees.

2. Melt butter in a pan over medium heat. Sauté garlic and onion until brown, about 8 minutes.

3. Stir in the pepper, salt, ½ a cup of cheddar cheese, spinach, feta, and mushrooms.

4. Pour into pie crust.

5. In a medium bowl, beat eggs and milk together lightly. Season with more salt & pepper and pour over vegetable mixture in pie crust.

6. Base in oven for 15 minutes. Sprinkle with the remaining cheese and bake an additional 40 minutes.

7. Serve and enjoy!

Hamburger Quiche

Adding hamburger to Quiche turns this normal brunch food into a hearty dinner. Filling and delicious, it will please all those at your dinner table!

Serving Size: 6 – 8

Total Prep Time: 1 hour 5 minutes

Ingredients:

- 1 – 16 oz. package frozen hash browns, thawed
- ½ lb. ground beef
- 1 onion, chipped
- 1 c. milk
- 2 eggs, lightly beaten
- 1 tbsp. cornstarch
- ½ lb. sharp cheddar, grated
- ¼ tsp. liquid smoke
- 1 – 3 oz. jar bacon bits
- 2 tsp. Worcestershire sauce
- ¼ lb. cheddar cheese, grated

Directions:

1. Preheat oven to 350 degrees and lightly grease 9" pie dish

2. Press hash browns into pie dish tightly and bake for 25 minutes in oven.

3. Put ground beef and onion in a large pan. Cook until beef evenly browns. Drain and allow to cool.

4. In a bowl, whisk together milk, eggs and cornstarch. Stir in the ½ lb. shredded cheese and ground beef. Stir in bacon bits, liquid smoke, and Worcestershire sauce.

5. Pour over hash browns

6. Bake for 20 minutes in oven, remove and sprinkle remaining cheese. Put back oven for 15 minutes. Let stand 20 minutes before serving.

7. Eat and enjoy!

wwwwwwwwwwwwwwwwwwwwwwwwwwwwwwwwwwwwww

Carrot Cashew Quiche

This recipe is very unique and combines delectable flavors that will impress any crowd. Serve it hot or cold and add a crisp salad for a light meal sure to please.

Serving Size: 6 – 8

Total Prep Time: 50 minutes

Ingredients:

- ½ c. butter
- 1 c. sliced carrots
- 1 c. cashews
- ½ c. honey
- 3 eggs
- 1 ½ c. heavy cream
- ½ tsp. nutmeg
- ½ tsp. salt
- ¾ c. shredded cheddar cheese
- 1 – 9" pie crust

Directions:

1. Preheat oven to 350 degrees

2. Add your butter in a pan over medium heat then stir in your cashews and carrots. Cook until your cashews are golden and carrots are tender. Mix in honey.

3. Whisk together heavy cream, salt, nutmeg and eggs.

4. Create a thin layer of cheese on the bottom of the pie crust. Place carrot mixture on top of cheese and add egg mixture.

5. Bake 40 minutes.

6. Serve & enjoy!

Bean Pie

This makes 2 pies that can be used at any time as a main dish or as a perfect party pie to be shared by a large group.

Serving Size: 6 - 8

Total Prep Time: 1 hour 30 minutes

Ingredients:

- 1 tbsp. vegetable oil
- 1 onion, chopped
- 1 green bell pepper, chopped
- 1 – 15 oz. can black beans, drained
- 1/3 c. salsa
- ¼ c. red bell pepper, chopped
- ¾ tsp. chili powder
- ¼ tsp cayenne pepper
- 2 – 9" pie shells
- 1 ½ c. cheddar cheese, grated

Directions:

1. Preheat oven to 325 degrees

2. Heat oil in a pan. Add onions and peppers and cook until tender. Stir in the beans, salsa, and seasonings and simmer for 15 minutes.

3. Spoon half into each pie crust and cover with cheese.

4. Bake for 1 hour!

Weeknight Quiche

This quiche is easy and fast. It uses crescent rolls as the crust for a light, flaky crust! Because it is not a traditional pie shell, cooking time is greatly reduced.

Serving Size: 6 – 8

Total Prep Time: 45 minutes

Ingredients:

- 1 – 8 oz. package crescent roll dough
- 2 slices ham
- ½ c. roasted red peppers, chopped
- 1 – 10 oz. package frozen spinach, chopped and thawed
- ½ c. shredded cheddar cheese
- 6 eggs
- 3 tbsp. milk
- Salt & Pepper to taste
- 1 splash hot sauce

Directions:

1. Heat oven to 350 degrees

2. Unroll the crescent dough into one piece. Line an 8x8 baking dish (it will extend over slightly). Prick the dough throughout with a fork.

3. Bake crust in oven about 10 minutes until golden

4. Layer the ham, peppers, spinach and cheese over the crust. Beat eggs, milk, salt & pepper and hot sauce in a bowl and pour into the pan.

5. Bake for 15 minutes. Turn oven to broil and cook for a few minutes more until top is slightly browned.

6. Cool and enjoy!

wwwwwwwwwwwwwwwwwwwwwwwwwwwwwwwwwwwwwww

Cheddar Quiche

This quiche is easy and delicious. With simple ingredients, a small kick of flavor, and a shorter baking time, it is a great one to use as a quick family dinner that the kids will love.

Serving Size: 6 – 8

Total Prep Time: 45 minutes

Ingredients:

- 1 – 9" frozen pie crust, unbaked
- 3 slices bacon, chopped
- 1 onion, chopped
- 2 c. shredded cheddar cheese
- 4 eggs
- 1 tsp. salt
- ¼ tsp. hot pepper sauce
- 1 – 12 oz. can evaporated milk, heated through

Directions:

1. Heat oven to 400 degrees.

2. Place bacon and onion in a skillet over medium heat and cook until bacon is browned. Drain and crumble the bacon into the pie shell. Add onions and cheddar cheese.

3. In a bowl, beat eggs with the salt and hot sauce and slowly stir in evaporated milk. Pour into the pie pan.

4. Bake 5 minutes, and then reduce heat to 350 degrees and bake for 25 minutes. The quiche will set more as it cools.

5. Enjoy!

wwwwwwwwwwwwwwwwwwwwwwwwwwwwwwwwwwwww

Beef & Biscuit Pie

With biscuits, ground beef, and onion this dish is the definition of savory. Substitute cheese flavorings to mix up the flavor.

Serving Size: 6 - 8

Total Prep Time: 45 minutes

Ingredients:

- 1 ¼ lb. ground beef
- ½ c. onion, chopped
- ¼ c. green chile peppers, chopped
- 1 – 8 oz. can tomato sauce
- 2 tsp. chili powder
- ½ tsp. garlic salt
- 1 – 10 oz. can buttermilk biscuit dough
- ½ c. sour cream
- 1 ½ c. Monterey Jack cheese, shredded & divided
- 1 egg beaten

Directions:

1. Preheat to 375 degrees

2. Brown ground beef, onion and green chili peppers in a pan. Add in the tomato sauce, chili powder and garlic. Mix and bring to simmer.

3. Pull the biscuits apart into 10 biscuits, and then pull each biscuit in half. Place 10 halves on the bottom of a pie dish to form the bottom crust.

4. Ad ½ c. cheese, sour cream and egg to meat mixture and then pour over crust. Add the last biscuit halves to the top in a layer. Sprinkle remaining cheese on top.

5. Bake for 30 minutes.

6. Enjoy!

Corn Tortilla Quiche

This quiche has a crispy tortilla crust that gives it a feel of a taco with the taste of a quiche. Delicious for any meal of the day, it is easy and fun to make!

Serving Size: 6 – 8

Total Prep Time: 1 hour

Ingredients:

- ¾ lb. bulk pork sausage
- 5 – 6" corn tortillas
- 1 c. shredded Monterey Jack cheese
- 1 c. shredded Cheddar cheese
- ¼ c. chopped green chilis
- 6 eggs, lightly beaten
- ½ c. heavy whipping cream
- ½ c. ricotta cheese
- ½ tsp. chili powder
- ¼ c. fresh cilantro, chopped

Directions:

1. Preheat oven to 350 degrees and lightly grease 9" pie dish

2. Cook sausage in skillet over high heat until crumbly and brown. Drain grease.

3. Place 4 tortillas in pie plate, overlap them ½ inch past the edge of the pan. Place final tortilla in center of pan. Place sausage, cheese, and green chilies over the tortillas.

4. Whisk eggs, cream, ricotta cheese and chili powder together and pour over the sausage mixture.

5. Bake about 45 minutes until center is set.

6. Sprinkle with cilantro and enjoy!

Chiles Rellenos Pie

You will find this warm and comforting in the winter but light enough for a summer dinner! Delicious Mexican flavor will make this a dinner favorite.

Serving Size: 6 - 8

Total Prep Time: 1 hour 5 minutes

Ingredients:

- 6 poblano chile peppers
- 2 c. Monterey jack cheese, grated
- 2 c. cheddar cheese, grated
- 1 ½ c. cooked chicken, diced
- 4 tbsp. flour
- 1 c. evaporated milk
- 1 c. sour cream
- 3 eggs
- 2 c. salsa

Directions:

1. Preheat oven on boiler setting. Roast the poblano chilis on a cookie sheet until the skin is charred on all sides.

2. Cool and peel off skin. Remove the stem and seeds. Turn oven temperature to 350 degrees.

3. Line an 11" baking dish with the peppers. Add cheeses evenly over the peppers. Spread the cooked chicken on top.

4. Mix the flour with a small amount of the evaporated milk until a paste forms, then whisk in the remaining milk and sour cream. Beat in eggs. Pour over the chicken.

5. Bake for 40 minutes and spread salsa on the top. Bake an additional 15 minutes.

6. Enjoy!

wwwwwwwwwwwwwwwwwwwwwwwwwwwwwwwwwwwww

Crab Quiche

This Crab Quiche can be delicious for brunch or even a tasteful dinner! Real or imitation crab meat can be used and the hot sauce can be adjusted to your tastes!

Serving Size: 6 – 8

Total Prep Time: 1 hour 15 minutes

Ingredients:

- 1 – 9" frozen pie crust
- 4 eggs
- 1 c. heavy cream
- ½ tsp salt
- ½ tsp pepper
- Hot Sauce – optional amount
- 1 c. shredded Monterey Jack cheese
- ¼ c. shredded parmesan cheese
- 1 – 8 oz. package of crab meat
- 1 green onion, diced

Directions:

1. Preheat oven to 350

2. Bake the pie crust for 10 minutes & remove

3. In a bowl, whisk the eggs, cream, salt and pepper and hot sauce.

4. Stir in cheese, onion and crab.

5. Pour into the pie shell and bake for 30 minutes in oven.

6. Turn off the oven, but leave the door closed and quiche in place for an additional 20 minutes. This makes for a creamier texture!

7. Serve & Enjoy

wwwwwwwwwwwwwwwwwwwwwwwwwwwwwwwwwwwwwww

Ham & Wild Rice Quiche

This recipe makes a change up from normal quiche with lots of veggies and wild rice. It's unique flavor makes it a great meal at any time.

Serving Size: 6 - 8

Total Prep Time: 55 minutes

Ingredients:

- 1 c. cooked wild rice
- 1 – 9" unbaked pie crust
- 1 c. cubed ham, cooked
- 1/3 c. red bell pepper, chopped
- ¼ c. green onion tops, sliced
- 1 – 4 oz. can mushroom, sliced
- 3 eggs, beaten
- 1 c. sour cream
- 1 tbsp. Dijon mustard
- ½ tsp. salt
- 1/8 tsp. pepper
- 2 c. Swiss cheese, shredded

Directions:

1. Preheat oven to 425 degrees. Bake pie crust 10 minutes and then reduce heat to 400.

2. Mix the rice, ham, peppers, onions and mushrooms in a bowl. Separately, mix eggs, sour cream, mustard and seasonings.

3. Place 1 c. swiss cheese in pie crust. Spread the rice, ham and veggie mix over the top and cover with the egg mixture. Top with remaining cheese.

4. Bake 30 minutes and remove. Let stand 10 minutes.

5. Serve & Enjoy!

Mexi-Quiche

Refried beans and a chorizo layer give this quiche a Mexican food twist that is delicious and unexpected. You can heat the beans slightly beforehand to make spreading easy.

Serving Size: 6 – 8

Total Prep Time: 55 minutes

Ingredients:

- 1 – 9" pie crust
- 6 eggs
- ¼ c. milk
- 1 – 10 oz. can tomatoes diced with green chili peppers
- 10 oz. of chorizo sausage
- 2 c. Mexican shredded cheese, divided
- 1 – 15 oz. can refried beans

Directions:

1. Preheat oven to 400.

2. Heat a pan over medium heat. Cook chorizo until brown and crumbly. Drain grease.

3. Beat eggs and milk in a bowl. Stir in tomato mixture and half the cheese.

4. Spread the beans across the bottom of the pie crust.

5. Spread chorizo on top of the refried beans and then pour egg mixture on top. Spread remaining cheese on top of the mixture.

6. Bake about 45 minutes, until toothpick inserted into middle comes out clean.

7. Let stand for 15 minutes before serving.

8. Enjoy!

wwwwwwwwwwwwwwwwwwwwwwwwwwwwwwwwwwwwwww

Morel Quiche

Morel mushrooms give this quiche a unique flavor. With heavy whipping cream, it is a fluffy and delicious meal at any time!

Serving Size: 6 – 8

Total Prep Time: 1 hour 17 minutes

Ingredients:

- 1 – 9" pie crust
- 1 tbsp. butter
- 1 onion, chopped
- ½ c. cooked ham, chopped
- 1 c. morel mushrooms
- 4 eggs
- 1 c. heavy whipping cream
- 1 tbsp. flour
- ½ c. Monterey jack cheese, shredded

Directions:

1. Preheat oven to 350

2. Heat butter in a pan until melted. Mix in onion and ham until onion is tender, about 5 minutes. Stir in mushrooms and cook, stirring frequently, for 2 minutes.

3. Bake pie crust in oven for approx. 10 minutes, until slightly browned.

4. Whisk eggs with cream and flour until mixed. Stir in cheese.

5. Spread ham and mushroom combination into pie crust and pour egg mixture on top.

6. Bake for 45 minutes until the filling is set!

wwwwwwwwwwwwwwwwwwwwwwwwwwwwwwwwwwwww

Cauliflower Cheese Pie

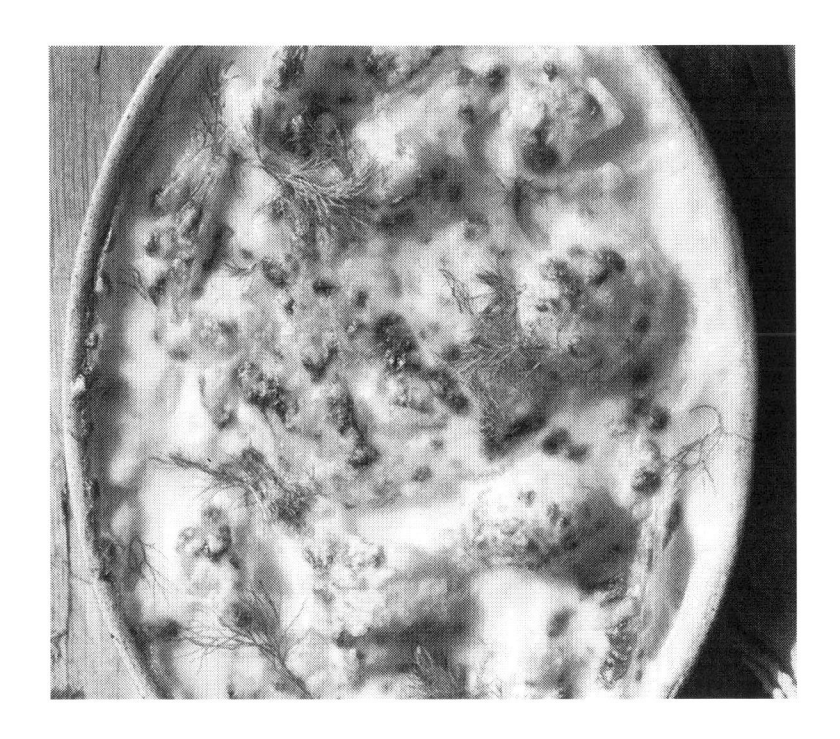

This recipe makes cauliflower extremely flavorful and delicious! With a potato crust it is a filling and healthy meal.

Serving Size: 6 - 8

Total Prep Time: 1 hour 40 minutes

Ingredients:

- 2 c. shredded potatoes
- ¼ c. onion, chopped
- 1 egg, beaten
- 1 tsp. salt
- 1 tbsp. flour
- 1 ½ tbsp. olive oil
- 1 tbsp. vegetable oil
- 1 onion, chopped
- 2 tsp garlic, minced
- ½ tsp. basil
- ½ tsp. thyme
- 1 head cauliflower, chopped
- 1 ½ c. cheddar cheese, grated
- 2 eggs, beaten
- ¼ c. milk
- ¼ tsp. paprika

Directions:

1. Preheat oven to 400 degrees and grease a 9" pie plate

2. In a bowl, combine potatoes, onion, egg, salt and flour. Transfer into pie pan and press firmly.

3. Bake for 30 minutes. Brush with oil and bake an additional 10 minutes. Remove and reduce oven heat to 375 degrees.

4. In a pan, heat oil and sauté onion, garlic basil and thyme with paprika until softened. Add cauliflower and cook for 15 minutes.

5. Spread ½ of the cheese onto the crust, then spread the vegetables on top. Add remaining cheese on top. Mix the milk and eggs and then pour over the top of the mixture.

6. Bake for 35 to 40 minutes and enjoy!

Vegetable Quiche

This Quiche is made for vegetarians. It provides a great light breakfast or lunch and can be served hot or cold!

Serving Size: 6 – 8

Total Prep Time: 1 hour 20 minutes

Ingredients:

- 1 tsp. salt
- ½ c. zucchini, chopped
- 1 – 9" pie crust, unbaked
- 2 tbsp. butter
- 1 ½ c. onion, chopped
- 1 green bell pepper, chopped
- 1 c. tomatoes, chopped
- ½ c. mushrooms, sliced
- 1 tsp. garlic, minced
- ¼ tsp. curry powder
- Salt & Pepper to taste
- ¼ tsp. ground cinnamon
- 5 eggs
- ¼ c. milk
- ¼ c. parmesan cheese, shredded
- ¼ c. cheddar cheese, shredded

Directions:

1. Sprinkle tsp. of salt over zucchini and let sit to drain for 10 minutes.

2. Preheat oven to 350.

3. Bake pie shell for 10 minutes

4. Melt butter in pan over medium heat. Cook onion, green peppers, tomatoes, mushrooms zucchini and minced garlic until tender. Stir in curry powder, salt & pepper, cinnamon and transfer into the pie crust.

5. Beat the eggs in a bowl with milk and all cheese. Pour over the vegetables.

6. Bake for 40 – 45 minutes. Let stand for 5 minutes before serving.

7. Enjoy!

Crustless Quiche

This healthier version of a quiche allows the delicious flavors without the added calories and carbs of a crust. Adjust ingredients to your taste and enjoy!

Serving Size: 6 - 8

Total Prep Time: 1 hour

Ingredients:

- 1 ½ tsp. olive oil
- 5 green onions, diced
- 2 tsp garlic, minced
- 1 – 6 oz bag baby spinach
- 1 ½ tsp. olive oil
- 8 mushrooms, sliced
- 4 eggs, whisked
- 8 oz. feta cheese, crumbled
- 1 lb. spicy cheese, shredded

Directions:

1. Preheat oven to 325 degrees.

2. Heat 1 ½ tsp oil in an oven safe pan. Cook green onions and garlic in oil for 1 minute. Stir in spinach, cover and cook about 5 minutes. Transfer to a large bowl

3. Heat 1 ½ tsp. oil in the same pan and cook mushrooms until lightly browned. Remove from heat.

4. Squeeze your spinach to remove any excess liquid. Stir into mushrooms.

5. Add whisked eggs to your spinach mixture. Stir in spicy cheese, and feta.

6. Transfer mixture back into pan. Bake in the oven for about 45 minutes.

7. Cut and enjoy!

wwwwwwwwwwwwwwwwwwwwwwwwwwwwwwwwwwwww

BBQ Pie

With baked beans and ground beef all under a crust, this dish is a perfect summer recipe to share with the whole family!

Serving Size: 6 - 8

Total Prep Time: 55 minutes

Ingredients:

- 1 ½ lbs. ground beef
- ¼ c. onion, chopped
- ¼ tsp. pepper
- 2 – 15 oz. cans baked beans with pork
- 1 tsp. Worcestershire sauce
- 1 c. BBQ sauce
- 1 c. biscuit baking mix
- ½ c. milk
- 1 egg
- ¼ c. cheddar cheese, shredded
- 1 tbsp. BBQ sauce

Directions:

1. Preheat oven to 350 degrees

2. Brown ground beef in a skillet with onion and pepper. Drain grease.

3. Stir in your BBQ sauce, Worcestershire sauce and baked beans. Place in a casserole dish. Separately, mix your egg, milk and baking mix. Pour on top of your beef mixture.

4. Bake for 45 minutes. Top with a bit of BBQ sauce, sprinkle with cheddar cheese while hot.

5. Enjoy!

wwwwwwwwwwwwwwwwwwwwwwwwwwwwwwwwwwww

Onion Quiche

This Quiche provides a tasty but versatile flavor. It can be used as a base for other quiches, a side dish for just about any meal, or a great meal on its own.

Serving Size: 6 – 8

Total Prep Time: 45 minutes

Ingredients:

- 1 – 9" frozen pie crust
- 1 tbsp. butter
- 1 onion, diced
- 3 eggs
- 1/3 c. heavy cream
- 1/3 c. shredded swiss cheese

Directions:

1. Preheat oven to 375

2. Melt butter in a saucepan. Add the onions and then cook until soft, about 5-6 minutes

3. In a bowl, mix the eggs and cream. Stir in the cheese.

4. Spread the onions over the bottom of the pie crust and pour the egg mixture over the onions.

5. Bake for 30 minutes.

6. Serve & Enjoy!

wwwwwwwwwwwwwwwwwwwwwwwwwwwwwwwwww

Quiche Seville

This quiche is easy and sophisticated. With bacon and sour cream mixed in, it produces a flavor that everyone will be sure to love.

Serving Size: 6 – 8

Total Prep Time: 1 hour 15 minutes

Ingredients:

- 1 – 9" pie crust, thawed
- 1 c. sour cream
- 10 slices bacon, crumbed
- 1 c. shredded Monterey Jack cheese
- 2 ¾ oz french fried dried onions
- 6 eggs, lightly beaten
- ½ tsp. Worcestershire sauce

Directions:

1. Preheat oven to 375 degrees

2. Bake pie shell for 10 minutes, then remove and reduce oven to 350 degrees.

3. In a bowl, combine sour cream, bacon, cheese, French-fried onions, Worcestershire sauce, and eggs together. Once mixed well, pour into the cooled pie shell.

4. Bake for 35 to 45 minutes until center is set.

5. Serve & Enjoy!

wwwwwwwwwwwwwwwwwwwwwwwwwwwwwwwwwwww

Tomato, Kale & Leek Quiche

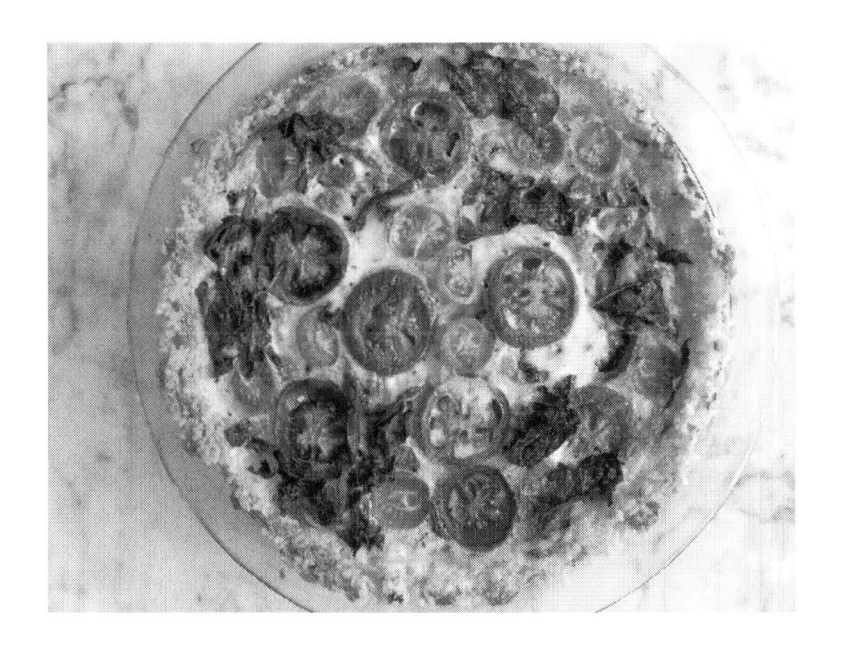

For the health lover, this crustless quiche is filled with vitamins from veggies. Make it at night and reheat for an easy, healthy breakfast.

Serving Size: 6 - 8

Total Prep Time: 1 hour

Ingredients:

- 1 c. kale, chopped & steamed
- 1 leek, sliced (green & white parts only)
- 4 oz. cherry tomatoes, halved
- 4 eggs
- 1 c. milk
- 4 oz. Italian Cheese mix, shredded
- 1 sprig rosemary, chopped
- ¼ tsp. salt
- 1 tbsp. parmesan cheese, shredded

Directions:

1. Preheat oven to 375 degrees. Grease an 8" pie crust

2. Place cooked kale in pie crust. Add sliced leek and the tomatoes.

3. In a bowl, mix eggs with milk and Italian cheese. Then stir in rosemary and salt.

4. Pour eggs over veggies in pie dish. Stir until the two mixtures are combined.

5. Bake about 30 minutes. Remove and top with parmesan cheese. Continue to bake for 20 more minutes.

6. Serve and Enjoy!

wwwwwwwwwwwwwwwwwwwwwwwwwwwwwwwwwwwwww

Easy Pot Pie

This may be the easiest version of pot pie available. Throw this together anytime you need a warm dinner in a flash.

Serving Size: 6 - 8

Total Prep Time: 25 minutes

Ingredients:

- 3 tbsp. butter, melted
- 1 -1 6 oz. package frozen veggie mix
- 1 – 5 oz. can chicken chunks (drained)
- 2 – 10.75 oz. cans cream of chicken soup
- ½ c. milk
- 1 – 10 oz. can layer biscuits

Directions:

1. Preheat to 425 degrees. Butter a pie dish with melted butter, reserving 1 tbsp.

2. Cook vegetables and chicken in a pan over medium heat until tender. Add soup and milk. Mix until well combined and smooth. Bring to a boil.

3. Take off stove and spread into the pie pan. Place the biscuits in small layers on top of mixture. Drizzle the remaining butter on top.

4. Bake for 15 minutes.

5. Enjoy!

wwwwwwwwwwwwwwwwwwwwwwwwwwwwwwwwwwwwwww

Rice Crust for Quiche

If you are looking for a healthier and unique crust to substitute in any quiche recipe, use this delicious rice crust as your base!

Serving Size: 1- 9" pie crust

Total Prep Time: 40 minutes

Ingredients:

- 1 c. water
- 1 c. instant rice
- 1 tbsp. butter
- Cooking spray

Directions:

1. Boil water in a small saucepan. Add rice, and cover. Allow to stand, off the heat, until water is absorbed, about 5 minutes. Stir in butter.

2. Grease a 9" pie pan. Spoon the rice into the pan. Press the rice firmly against the pan with the back of your spoon to create a crust.

3. Fill with quiche recipe of your choice and bake as directed! Enjoy!

wwwwwwwwwwwwwwwwwwwwwwwwwwwwwwwwwwwww

Salmon Quiche

For those who don't love turkey or ham, this salmon dish can easily be a delicious substitute. You can make 2 and freeze one for later! Serve with fresh veggies like asparagus for an amazing dinner.

Serving Size: 6 – 8

Total Prep Time: 45 minutes

Ingredients:

- 1 – 9" pie crust, thawed
- 1 – 8 oz. package cheddar cheese block. Cubed.
- ¼ onion, chopped
- 4 eggs
- 1 – 12 fluid oz. can evaporated milk
- Salt & Pepper to taste
- ¼ tsp. garlic powder
- ¼ tsp. dried parsley
- ¼ tsp. dried sage
- 1 – 14.75 oz can salmon, drained, remove bones
- ½ c. shredded cheddar cheese, divided

Directions:

1. Preheat oven to 375 degrees

2. Place cubed cheddar cheese, onion, eggs and milk into blender. Add seasonings and blend until smooth and mixed.

3. Spread salmon into pie crust. Sprinkle ¼ c. shredded cheddar cheese over the salmon, and pour the egg mixture in. Top with remaining cheese.

4. Bake for 30 minutes, or until set

5. Serve & Enjoy!

wwwwwwwwwwwwwwwwwwwwwwwwwwwwwwwww

Bacon Pie

A bacon pie can be eaten at breakfast, lunch or dinner for a savory and tasty meal.

Serving Size: 6 - 8

Total Prep Time: 55 minutes

Ingredients:

- 12 slices bacon
- 1 c. swiss cheese, grated
- 1/3 c. onion, chopped
- 2 c. milk
- 4 eggs
- 1 c. baking mix
- 1/8 tsp. black pepper

Directions:

1. Heat oven to 400 degrees. Grease a 9" pie plate

2. Cook bacon until brown, drain & dry and crumble.

3. Spread bacon, cheese and onion into the dish.

4. Mix the milk, eggs and baking mix with pepper in a small bowl. Pour over the bacon mixture.

5. Bake 40 minutes.

6. Serve and enjoy!

Shrimp Quiche

This can be made on its own or as an accompaniment to the prior Salmon Quiche for a seafood quiche buffet! It can be served cold or hot.

Serving Size: 6 – 8

Total Prep Time: 40 minutes

Ingredients:

- 1 – 9" pie crust, baked
- 4 oz. small cooked shrimp (peeled & deveined)
- 2/3 c. Gruyere Cheese
- 2 eggs, lightly beaten
- 1 c. sour cream
- 1 tbsp. green onion, chopped
- Salt & Pepper

Directions:

1. Preheat oven to 350 degrees

2. Spread shrimp across pie crust and sprinkle with cheese

3. Stir the sour cream, onion and salt and pepper into the eggs and pour over the cheese/shrimp

4. Bake for 30 minutes

5. Serve and enjoy!

wwwwwwwwwwwwwwwwwwwwwwwwwwwwwwwwwwww

Spinach Artichoke Quiche

The artichoke in this recipe adds a delicious, almost tart flavor to the recipe. The full tomato slices create a beautiful dish that will look good on any table.

Serving Size: 6 - 8

Total Prep Time: 1 hour

Ingredients:

- 1 – 9" unbaked pie shell
- 4 eggs
- 5 slices bacon, cooked & crumbled
- ½ c. mozzarella cheese, shredded
- 2 tbsp. milk
- 2 tbsp. flour
- 2 tsp. garlic, minced
- 1 tsp. parsley
- ½ tsp. thyme
- 1 c. spinach, divided
- ½ c. artichoke hearts, chopped
- 2 plum tomatoes, sliced

Directions:

1. Preheat oven to 350 degrees.

2. Mix eggs, bacon, mozzarella, milk, flour, and spices together.

3. Place ½ of spinach on bottom of pie crust. Sprinkle the artichoke hearts over the spinach. Pour eggs on top. Place remaining spinach over eggs, and top with tomato slices.

4. Bake about 45 minutes until center is set.

5. Enjoy!

Chicken Pot Pie

This pie made from scratch will impress any company! It is hearty, savory and filling and a perfect meal for a winter or fall evening.

Serving Size: 6 - 8

Total Prep Time: 1 hour 15 minutes

Ingredients:

- 1 lb. skinless/boneless chicken breast, cubed
- 1 c. carrots, sliced
- 1 c. frozen green peas
- ½ c. celery, chopped
- 1/3 c. butter
- 1/3 c. onion, diced
- 1/3 c. flour
- ½ tsp. salt
- ¼ tsp. pepper
- ¼ tsp. celery seed
- 1 ¾ c. chicken broth
- 2/3 c. milk
- 2 -9" pie crusts

Directions:

1. Set your oven to preheat to 425 degrees

2. Place celery, peas, carrots and chicken into a large saucepan. Cover with water and boil for 15 minutes. Drain and set mixture aside

3. In the same pan, cook butter and onions until soft. Stir in your celery seeds, and flour then season to taste. Slowly mix in your milk and broth. Simmer until thick. Remove from heat.

4. Place the chicken mixture in one pie crust. Pour the broth mixture on top. Cover with the second pie crust. Seal edges and make small slits in the top to vent.

5. Bake for 35 minutes. Cook for 10 minutes.

6. Serve & Enjoy!

wwwwwwwwwwwwwwwwwwwwwwwwwwwwwwwwwwww

Ultimate Quiche

This quiche is very creamy and filling. It can be frozen for later after baking, and any combination of meats that you can think of can be used or substituted.

Serving Size: 6 – 8

Total Prep Time: 1 hour 30 minutes

Ingredients:

- 1 – 9" frozen pie crust, unbaked
- 1 ½ tsp. green bell pepper, chopped
- ½ onion, diced
- ¼ c. mushrooms, chopped
- 3 eggs
- 1 c. heavy cream
- ¼ lb. shredded Monterey Jack cheese
- ¼ lb. shredded Swiss cheese
- 6 oz. cooked ham, chopped
- ¼ tsp. vinegar
- ¼ tsp. tarragon
- Pinch of garlic powder
- Pinch of ground nutmeg
- Salt & Pepper to taste

Directions:

1. Heat oven to 350 degrees and cook pie crust for 10 minutes

2. In a pan, sauté green pepper, onions and mushroom until translucent

3. In a large bowl, mix eggs and cream. Add in cheeses, ham and sautéed vegetables. Stir in the vinegar and season with herbs. Pour into pie crust

4. Bake for 55 to 60 minutes

5. Serve and enjoy!

wwwwwwwwwwwwwwwwwwwwwwwwwwwwwwwwwwwwwww

Artichoke Pie

You can use this recipe for a main dish or an appetizer. It is always enjoyed and is very easy to make at any time!

Serving Size: 6 - 8

Total Prep Time: 1 hour 15 minutes

Ingredients:

- 1 tbsp. olive oil
- 1 tsp. garlic, minced
- 2 – 6 oz. cans artichoke hearts
- ½ c. Italian bread crumbs
- ½ c. parmesan cheese, divided
- 1 9" pie crust
- 3 eggs, beaten
- 1 – 8 oz. package mozzarella cheese, grated

Directions:

1. Preheat oven to 350 degrees

2. Heat oil in a skillet and sauté garlic until it starts to brown. Add artichoke hearts and cook 10 minutes.

3. Add the bread crumbs and ½ the parmesan cheese. When heated all through and mixed, place half of the mixture into the crust.

4. Pour the eggs of the artichoke mixture and the rest of the parmesan cheese. Add the rest of the artichoke mixture and top with mozzarella.

5. Bake for 45 minutes!

Conclusion

You did it! Congratulations on cooking your way to the end of this Quiche Cookbook. Hopefully, you found all 30 of these tasty quiche recipes easy to follow and delicious! Now, with these 30 Quiche recipes added to your arsenal of meals, you should be able to mix and match the ingredients to create even other delicious creations that are all tasty and intriguing.

Be sure to leave us a review if you like what you read and that you will join us again for yet another delicious journey.

Until next time… Happy Cooking!

wwwwwwwwwwwwwwwwwwwwwwwwwwwwwwwwwwwwwwww

About the Author

Born in New Germantown, Pennsylvania, Stephanie Sharp received a Masters degree from Penn State in English Literature. Driven by her passion to create culinary masterpieces, she applied and was accepted to The International Culinary School of the Art Institute where she excelled in French cuisine. She has married her cooking skills with an aptitude for business by opening her own small cooking school where she teaches students of all ages.

Stephanie's talents extend to being an author as well and she has written over 400 e-books on the art of cooking and baking that include her most popular recipes.

Sharp has been fortunate enough to raise a family near her hometown in Pennsylvania where she, her husband and children live in a beautiful rustic house on an extensive piece of land. Her other passion is taking care of the furry members of her family which include 3 cats, 2 dogs and a potbelly pig named Wilbur.

Watch for more amazing books by Stephanie Sharp coming out in the next few months.

Author's Afterthoughts

I am truly grateful to you for taking the time to read my book. I cherish all of my readers! Thanks ever so much to each of my cherished readers for investing the time to read this book!

With so many options available to you, your choice to buy my book is an honour, so my heartfelt thanks at reading it from beginning to end!

I value your feedback, so please take a moment to submit an honest and open review on Amazon so I can get valuable insight into my readers' opinions and others can benefit from your experience.

Thank you for taking the time to review!

Stephanie Sharp

For announcements about new releases, please follow my author page on Amazon.com!

(Look for the Follow Bottom under the photo)

You can find that at:

https://www.amazon.com/author/stephanie-sharp

*or Scan **QR-code** below.*

Printed in Poland
by Amazon Fulfillment
Poland Sp. z o.o., Wrocław